RESETTING
for
SUCCESS

Discovering What You
Are Meant To Do

By Felecia C. Harris, EdD
with Kenya Redd & Tahnya Williams

Resetting for Success: Discovering What You Are
Meant To Do, Copyright© 2017 Felecia Harris

Published by Warren Publishing
ISBN: 978-1-943258-52-9

Printed in the United States of America

contents

1

You are a Miracle

11

Hit the Reset Button

15

Your Mess is a Message

23

Success is in Your DNA

30

Fear Factor

37

All In

" Is success about
learning or proving
how smart you are? "

Carol S. Dweck

A re you ready to reset for success? Understanding the question of whether success is about what you know or demonstrating how much you know has everything to do with succeeding at what you are meant to do.

Success is built on a number of variables. Malcolm Gladwell, in *Outliers* states that success is a combination of birth, timing, exposure to resources and privileges, and some occurrences that are not planned.

We all have our own measures of success. Examining successful people is one way to measure, but success can be defined at many different levels — there is no one right way. Success is about what you do on a daily basis for yourself — prayer, meditation, exercise, workshops, certifications, and sometimes just "nothing" so you have time to reflect.

Resetting for Success: Discovering What You Are Meant To Do, is a guide in taking the first steps on the path to success.

Breaking it Down

This book is split into six sections. "You are a Miracle" discusses how wonderfully made we all are and teaches us to look for the miracles in all aspects of our lives. Section two, "Hit the Reset Button," is designed to get you motivated toward taking that first step and reminding yourself that it is okay to venture into the unknown. Section three, "Your Mess Is a Message," teaches you how to not get discouraged when you can't immediately see the end you have in mind. Section four, "Success is in Your DNA," focuses on the fact that we are all wired for success. Fear can be the biggest barrier to doing what your are meant to do. Section five, "The Fear Factor" examines how to push past the anxieties associated with success. Finally, section six, "All In," explores how to focus and get motivated for change and success.

"Commit your actions to
the Lord and your plans
will succeed."

Proverbs 16:9 NLT

chapter one

"There are only two ways to live your life. One is as though nothing is a miracle. The other is as though everything is a miracle."

Albert Einstein

1

YOU ARE A MIRACLE
BY FELECIA HARRIS

Albert Einstein lived every day reminding himself that in order to be successful, he needed to give the same energy he received. Just like Einstein, you should live every day reminding yourself that you are a miracle and there is no one exactly like you.

A miracle is defined as an extraordinary or unusual event, thing, or accomplishment

1

manifesting from divine support. Miracles are seen in the extraordinary measures God uses to reveal himself to us, and they remind us that we are not dependent on our own abilities in order to accomplish the seemingly impossible. Miracles come into our lives with purpose and with timing. You may find yourself thinking:

• What's in front of me seems impossible!
• Why it is so difficult to climb this mountain?

But then it all comes together and is done, and you think, "That was a miracle!"

Resetting for Success: Discovering What You Are Meant To Do provides a way for us to see miracles in the midst of change, transitions, problems, or tragedies and have faith that something good is waiting around the corner. This book is designed to read all at once or read each section as it speaks to your individual needs. Managing change in our lives can be complex, so resources like this can assist in discovering the steps and strategies that will make your journey successful.

Do you know who you are?

Spend time learning who you are. This sounds so simple, but so many people fail to spend time getting to know themselves. When you know who you are, making changes becomes clearer.

When I first went to graduate school, I had this idea I wanted to be the president of a college. I would go through the traditional pathway of faculty, teaching, college administration, and then presidency. Straight out of school, I began my journey. I interviewed for several positions and finally found an administrative job. I stayed in that position for eight years, and during that time, I realized I did not want to be a college president and I did not like administration.

The first moment I knew what I wanted to do was when I was given the opportunity to lead a Ford Foundation Grant training session — and I loved it! I enjoyed interacting with individuals and delivering material that changed how they learned and mastered information that impacted their lives. I knew this was what I liked doing and I had the skills to do it well, so I transitioned to another training position that was grant-funded.

Knowing who you are and how you are gifted opens the door for what you are meant to do.

The job announcement was wonderfully written and I said to myself, "this is a great opportunity" — until my first day on the job. This new job was a Department of Education job, but 90% administration. It was in that moment I realized it was time to pursue training full-time. Still, I decided not leave the position immediately. I decided to complete this project while I looked for opportunities to teach and train.

The moment I declared what I truly wanted to do, I was met with an opportunity to provide diversity training to our entire unit. In addition, as I was waiting for the project to end, I received two more opportunities — my first corporate training project with a Fortune 500 company and a training project with the city of Charlotte.

Knowing who you are and how you are gifted opens the door for what you are meant to do.

"Everyone is unique and has a unique calling. Using this fingerprint of yourself in the service of others is the best way to succeed."

Oprah Winfrey

"Be yourself, everyone else is already taken."

Oscar Wilde

"You alone are enough."

Maya Angelou

chapter two

"Be the change you wish to see in the world."

Mahatma Gandhi

2

HIT THE RESET BUTTON
BY FELECIA HARRIS

You can remake your life from the inside out. Doing what you are meant to do requires doing things you have never done before — in ways you never could have imagined. In order to be successful, you must learn and practice skills you may not have realized you have. That is how you learn who you are!

Hitting the reset button is not always easy. Spending time discovering "who" you are is a great first step. Sounds easy, but for many of us, this process can be extremely challenging. Our lives are intertwined with so many responsibilities. Many of us are nurturers taking care of everyone else, and often that does not include ourselves.

Deciding to make a change requires accepting the unexpected.

Embarking on change, however, can open the door to creating new opportunities. Do not let doubt get in the way. Evaluate what you are doing and why.

Deciding to make a change requires accepting the unexpected and having faith your steps will lead you to what you are destined to do. Go for it.

Hit that reset button!

chapter three

"The past has no power
over the present moment.

Eckhart Tolle

3

YOUR MESS IS A MESSAGE
BY FELECIA HARRIS

When you are seeking to make a change, there is a tendency to try to make things "perfect;" everything has to be nice, neat, and in order. Unfortunately, changes do not normally come ordered or neatly-packaged.

When you examine what's going on in your life, you cannot see the end because it is made up of pieces — sort of like a recipe.

A cake requires ingredients like eggs, butter, vanilla extract, milk, and flour. If you try to eat these ingredients individually, they do not taste good, but when you mix them together the combination creates something delicious. Something special. Something successful.

Our lives are like that. We experience things in pieces. I spent ten years earning my education — and planned to be the next Ann Fudge, who, at the time, was the highest ranking African American female executive at General Mills Foods. I was going to be a great entrepreneur! I came up with a company name, created a website, and became incorporated. I even designed a brochure. At the same, time I was working as a university administrator, I

We experience things in pieces — I could not see the light at the end of the tunnel because there were pieces everywhere.

was married, and I had a six-month-old child. I was involved in entrepreneurial networking groups, and was working in the community. Working during the day, coming home, and then working half the night after my family was asleep was my ritual. I was attempting to stir all these elements together. What a mess!

When I look back on that time, I realize now it was like a big pile of unsorted clothes. I couldn't match my socks for all the shirts, pants, and towels!

That mess brought me to the point of sitting down and really thinking about my intentions. I realized traditional, full-time employment was

[My] mess brought me to the point of sitting down and really thinking about my intentions.

not what me nor my family needed. By this time, I had two children and just organizing the family schedule of picking the kids up from daycare was like managing a major corporation. I was always running around in the mess. However, as I got more intentional about what I was doing, my mess became a message to me, telling me who I was and what I was intended to be doing. Once I was clear on that, new opportunities came rushing through the door.

Understand that when you put your "mess" together, you can discover the "message" waiting for you.

"You can have it all, just not all at the same time."

Betty Friedan

"Success is not final,
failure is not fatal.
It is courage to
continue that counts."

Sir Winston Churchill

chapter four

“ Success is doing what
you want to do, when you
want, where you want,
with whom you want as
much as you want! ”

Tony Robins

4

SUCCESS IS IN YOUR DNA
BY TAHNYA WILLIAMS

CERTIFIED RELATIONSHIP AND LIFE COACH

Throughout my life, there have been times where I wondered "if only." If only I made this amount of money. If only I had this car or that house. It felt like if I were to achieve this or that, I would be what society considered "successful." Well, I have worked very hard, overcome many obstacles and failures, changed my state of mind, and achieved the goals I have set for myself.

Although I have become successful, this is just the beginning. This is not the end. This is not a place to stop and become complacent. I have the courage to continue and knock down successes like bowling pins.

Your life is more than an illusion. I became free over ten years ago. I was a slave to my life and to those who existed in it. I was shackled with experiences that I placed on myself and those around me. By all accounts, I was society's version of successful, but I was unhappy.

Your life is more than an illusion... I was society's version of successful, but I was unhappy.

Being a slave worked for me — for a while at least. I looked to others to direct my life in order to take the pressure, accountability, and responsibility off of me. I came face to face with my unhappiness as I sat in my overstuffed chair in the corner. Looking around the room, it hit me. The illusion of how I was living my life became crystal clear, as if I were looking at a life that was not my own. (Well it was my own, but I let others write the story for me.) I started thinking: *What if I just did what I wanted to do? What If I took a vacation? Just me, all by myself. What if I bought that car? What if I left the job that made me so dissatisfied? What if, in the moment, I did exactly what I wanted to do? What if I did something that made me happy with no thought of how it would affect others?* It sounds simple, but it was a freeing moment. A great sense of calmness and excitement came over me. It was what Oprah would call "the light bulb moment."

What if, in the moment, I did exactly what I wanted to do?

Why had I been living in a box, confined by others' expectations? The answer was my *fear* of making a change. My fear gripped me as if I were a frightened child in a dark room at night. In that moment, I decided I would no longer allow fear to control one more aspect of my life. On that day, I became free. I became *me*.

My journey of success is just beginning. Nothing stops me anymore. No one in my life dictates how I live my life, or who I choose to have in it. Nobody else decides where I choose to go or when and with whom, or what I choose to do for my career passion. Fear does not have a single crumb of control over any aspect of my life.

I am living!

"Success is a state of mind. If you choose success...start thinking of yourself as a success. "

Dr. Joyce Brothers

5

chapter five

"I have not failed. I've found 10,000 ways that won't work. "

Thomas Edison

5

FEAR FACTOR
BY KENYA REDD

MARKETING EXPERT WITH OVER
20 YEARS' EXPERIENCE IN THE
ENTERTAINMENT INDUSTRY

In the words of Franklin D. Roosevelt, "The only thing we have to fear is fear itself." Fear is the wall that keeps you from living the life of your dreams. Push beyond your own fears and turn a deaf ear to the naysayers.

The life of an entrepreneur is a slippery slope. It is not for the faint of heart. You see the lives of successful entrepreneurs, but you rarely hear about their pitfalls until they have made it to the point of what others deem to be success.

I have been in the realm of entertainment and marketing for twenty-three years. I did not realize how much owning my own business was truly in my DNA. When I was first starting out, I wrote and drew samples for greeting cards by hand. I did not go anywhere with it then, but now, due to the resources that are made readily available, I can easily start that venture if I choose to. I didn't fail, I just needed time. I do not believe in giving up. I go where my passion leads, and sometimes that means I get a few bumps and bruises. However, I have learned how to do something better for the next go-round.

"Do not let what you can't do interfere with what you can do."

John Woodson

We have all looked at someone else's life and tried to envision what it would be like to either be them or do what they do, anyone from an actress to a model, an architect to a magazine editor. But that is as far as we go. We immediately think we cannot run a multi-million dollar company or have that platinum album. Newsflash: yes you can!

We have all looked at someone else's life and tried to envision what it would be like to do what they do.

I wanted to be involved in the film and TV industry, so I began auditioning and landed small roles in a few major productions and lead roles in some indie projects. I gave things a try just to be a part in some way. I found that it was the production and screen playwriting aspect that appealed to me. I was more fulfilled being behind the scenes than in front of the camera.

With my company, I have found this: if there is something that needs to be done and I am unable to do it, I will find someone who is successful and enjoys doing that task. The more everyone is focused on what they have a passion for, the more successful the project will be.

If you think you can build an empire without a proper foundation and key individuals, you are mistaken. So you love film? Be a producer. You love the fashion world? Produce fashion events. Find what you love to do and do it. Find the right people to help you and don't let fear get in the way.

Move beyond your fear. Don't let it keep you from living the life of your dreams. Life is meant to be lived and enjoyed.

"Before I can tell my life what I want to do with it, I must listen to my life telling me who I am."

Parker Palmer

6 chapter six

"Life's biggest lessons
are within ourselves."

Eille Wiesel, Holocaust survivor

6

ALL IN
by FELECIA HARRIS

Explore change by setting high expectations for yourself. Be a self-fulfilling prophecy or a prediction that causes itself to become true. Being tenacious: (determination; persistence; perseverance) if you think and believe you can do it, you can. Success begins with believing.

I was watching an interview of Tyler Perry, and he was sharing how he started his first plays. Using his credit cards, he would put the plays together and no one would show up. He did this for five years, working, sometimes living in his car, putting his plays together and very small groups would show up. He lost all his money. Then, one night he walked up to the theater and the line was around the building. What did he do? He believed and kept moving forward.

Believe and keep moving forward.

How many books, businesses, or projects are never started or are left incomplete when we give up? If Tyler Perry had not stayed the course, we would not have the wonderful "Madea" to keep us laughing and thinking.

Being "all in" means chartering a course that is suited for you. The first step is to access information from role models and mentors. You can benefit from their models and wisdom, but ultimately your job is not to be a copy machine or replica of them. Your job is to recognize what *you* bring to the table. For example, according to Malcolm Gladwell, author of *Outliers*, it takes approximately 10,000 hours to master what you are meant to do. Take Oprah, for example. She makes interviewing people look so easy. But after interviewing 37,000 people over 25 years, any of us would be able to do that, too. Success means challenging yourself with the highest expectations and understanding it will take time to get there.

> *Your job is not to be a copy machine or replica of [your role models].*

"All in" means "closing doors" and leaving unnecessary things behind. One of my favorite examples of closing doors was shared by Bishop T.D. Jakes. He spoke about how often people are unable to move forward because they will not let go. He shared about how after he gave a speech in New York, he stayed at the Four Seasons Hotel. In order to go to private sections of the hotel, one had to go through two sets of doors. Bishop walked through the first set of doors and approached the second set and the doors would not open. So he backed up and walked through the first set of doors once more, then attempted to go through the second set of doors again. They still would not open. Finally, he backed up again, walked through the first set, and waited until they were completely closed. Then he moved forward toward the second set of doors and they opened wide.

"All in" means you may have to close some doors completely to reach the next level of success.

www.ingramcontent.com/pod-product-compliance
Lightning Source LLC
Chambersburg PA
CBHW021226020426
42331CB00003B/493